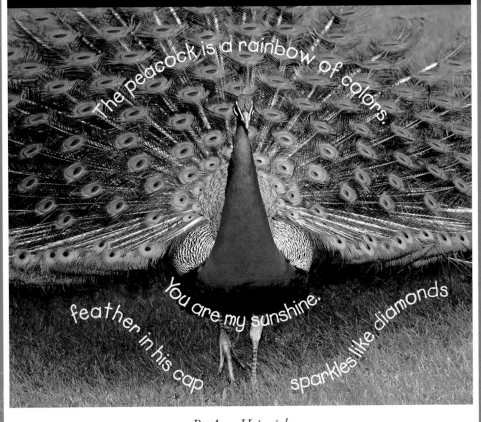

THE MAGIC OF LANGUAGE

Similes and Metaphors

By Ann Heinrichs

THE CHILD'S WORLD®
CHANHASSEN, MINNESOTA

The peacock is a rainbow of colors.

You are my sunshine.

feather in his cap

sparkles like diamonds

Time is money.

dropping like leaves

hard as a rock

blind as a bat

sly as a fox

hair like silk

The Child's World

Published in the United States of America by The Child's World®
PO Box 326, Chanhassen, MN 55317-0326
800-599-READ
www.childsworld.com

Content Adviser:
Kathy Rzany, MA,
Adjunct Professor,
School of Education,
Dominican University,
River Forest, Illinois

Photo Credits: Cover/frontispiece: Corbis. Interior: Corbis: 16 (Cheque), 18 (Roy Morsch), 25 (Tom Stewart), 26 (Matthew Klein), 29 (LWA-Dann Tardiff); Getty Images/The Image Bank: 17 (Steve Satushek), 23 (GK Hart/Vikki Hart); Getty Images/Photographer's Choice: 5 (Art Montes De Oca), 27 (Duncan Smith); Getty Images/Stone: 7 (Gabor Geissler), 14 (Ben Edwards), 21 (David Roth); Getty Images/Stone+/Ryan McVay: 22; Bonnie Kamin/PhotoEdit: 11; Joe McDonald/Corbis: 9, 13.

The Child's World®: Mary Berendes, Publishing Director

Editorial Directions, Inc.: E. Russell Primm, Editorial Director; Katie Marsico, Project Editor and Line Editor; Matt Messbarger, Editorial Assistant; Susan Hindman, Copyeditor; Sarah E. De Capua and Lucia Raatma, Proofreaders; Peter Garnham, Elizabeth Nellums, Olivia Nellums, Daisy Porter, and Will Wilson, Fact Checkers; Timothy Griffin/IndexServ, Indexer; Cian Loughlin O'Day, Photo Researcher; Linda S. Koutris, Photo Editor

The Design Lab: Kathleen Petelinsek, Art Direction; Kari Thornborough, Page Production

Library of Congress Cataloging-in-Publication Data
Heinrichs, Ann.
  Similes and metaphors / by Ann Heinrichs.
     p. cm. — (The magic of language)
  Includes index.
  ISBN 1-59296-434-6 (library bound : alk. paper) 1. Simile—Juvenile literature.
2. Metaphor—Juvenile literature. 3. Figures of speech—Juvenile literature. 4. English language—Style—Juvenile literature. I. Title.
  PE1445.S5H45 2006
  808—dc22   2005004008

TABLE OF CONTENTS

CHAPTER ONE

WHAT IS A SIMILE?

DEFINITION

A **simile** compares two things using **like** or **as**.

Suppose a bear went ice-skating. You could describe his adventure this way:

EXAMPLE

The bear was graceful. He seemed to float along. His smile was sweet.

But you could make the story much more interesting and funny. You could add phrases, or groups of words, to express your thoughts a different way.

These ballerinas are very graceful. Can you imagine a bear ice-skating like this? You can use a simile to say the bear is *as graceful as a ballerina.*

The bear was as graceful as a ballerina. He seemed to float along like a butterfly. His smile was as sweet as honey.

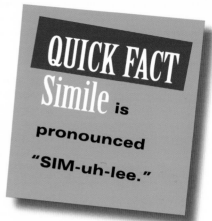

QUICK FACT

Simile is pronounced "SIM-uh-lee."

All the blue phrases in this example are similes. Similes work by comparing two things. Those two things are different in most ways. But they are alike in one important way. Here are the things being compared in the example:

EXAMPLE

SUBJECT	COMPARED TO	HOW THEY ARE ALIKE
bear	ballerina	Both are graceful.
bear	butterfly	Both float smoothly.
smile	honey	Both are sweet.

A simile is an interesting way of describing something. It can make a subject clearer. It can bring a subject to life or make it funny. After all, how could a bear ever be **like a butterfly?** Only in a simile!

TRY THESE!

Each sentence below contains a **simile**.
Name the two things being compared.
How are those two things alike?

1. Lauren was as quiet as a mouse.
2. The ocean was so smooth that it looked like glass.
3. Ben was stretching his neck like a giraffe.

See page 32 for the answers. Don't peek!

*Are you curious? Do you stretch your neck to get a better look at things? If you do, there's a simile just for you. You might be stretching your neck **like a giraffe!***

CHAPTER TWO

SIMILES USING LIKE

Some similes compare things by using the word **like.** A simile using **like** may modify, or describe, a verb. These similes usually answer the question "how?" Just look at the following examples:

EXAMPLE

Samantha's turtle sleeps like a log.
Richard eats like a bird.
My frog hops like a kangaroo.
Here comes a tiger. Run like the wind!

QUICK FACT
A verb is a word that shows action or being.

These similes all describe verbs, or action words. They tell *how* the action happened.

VERB (ACTION)	SIMILE (ANSWERS "HOW?")
sleeps	like a log
eats	like a bird
hops	like a kangaroo
run	like the wind

Some similes use **like** to describe nouns. These similes often follow

a linking verb. Here are some examples:

EXAMPLE

These cookies taste like sawdust!
That flamingo stands like a statue.
A stuffed animal is like an old friend.

*What a big hop! Does this frog hop **like a kangaroo**? Or **like a grasshopper**?*

All these similes describe nouns.

A linking verb joins each simile to the

word it describes.

EXAMPLE

SUBJECT	LINKING VERB	SIMILE (DESCRIBES SUBJECT)
These cookies	**taste**	**like sawdust**
That flamingo	**stands**	**like a statue**
The stuffed animal	**is**	**like an old friend**

TRY THESE!

Write three sentences about someone you know. Include a simile that uses like in each sentence.

See page 32 for the answers. Don't peek!

CHAPTER THREE

SIMILES USING AS

EXAMPLE

After the race, Clare's legs were **as limp as noodles.**

My new blue blanket is **as soft as a kitten.**

Daniel was so scared that his eyes were **as big as saucers.**

Mary had a little lamb. Its fleece was **white as snow.**

All these similes use **as** to compare two things. The two things are alike in one important way.

These boys must be amazed by something on their computer.
*Their eyes are **as big as saucers**!*

SUBJECT	COMPARED TO	HOW THEY ARE ALIKE
legs	noodles	Both are limp.
blanket	kitten	Both are soft.
eyes	saucers	Both are big.
fleece	snow	Both are white.

Want More?

Here are more common **similes** using **as:**

as clear as a bell

as cold as ice

as cool as a cucumber

as cute as a button

as dry as a bone

as easy as ABC

as flat as a pancake

as good as gold

as light as a feather

as quick as a wink

as smooth as silk

as solid as a rock

as tight as a drum

CHAPTER FOUR

BLIND AS A BAT,
SLY AS A FOX

Many similes use **as** to compare something to an animal.

Have you heard any of these animal similes before?

*People sometimes use the simile **blind as a bat**. But bats aren't really blind.*
They just rely on their big ears to locate things!

*Are you **as strong as an ox**? People use oxen such as these to carry or pull heavy loads.*

as blind **as a** bat

as brave **as a** lion

as busy **as a** beaver

as busy **as a** bee

as free **as a** bird

as proud **as a** peacock

as slow **as a** snail

as sly **as a** fox

as strong **as an** ox

as stubborn **as a** mule

as wise **as an** owl

CHAPTER FIVE

REALLY LONG SIMILES

A simile compares two things. Those two things can be more than one-word objects. They can be entire activities. This kind of simile can be pretty funny. Here are some examples:

EXAMPLE

Studying math is like beating my head against a brick wall.

Looking for Janna in the mall is like looking for a needle in a haystack.

Brushing dirt off this floor is like sweeping sand off the seashore.

I'm grounded all week. I feel like a bug trapped in a jar.

People swarmed around the singer like ants on a box of doughnuts.

When Matt talks to Katie, he's as nervous as a long-tailed cat in a room full of rocking chairs.

*These twins are **as alike as two peas in a pod**.*

TRY THESE!

Think of sentences using these similes:

as plain as the nose on your face

as snug as a bug in a rug

as alike as two peas in a pod

as welcome as flowers in May

as easy as falling off a log

See page 32 for the answers. Don't peek!

CHAPTER SIX

SIMILE JOKES

Similes can make good jokes. They compare things that are *extremely* different.

These kids are laughing about one of the simile jokes on the next page. Which joke do you think is the funniest?

Just look at these examples:

QUESTION: **When is a door like a bottle?**
ANSWER: **When it's ajar.**

QUESTION: **When is a boat like a pile of snow?**
ANSWER: **When it's adrift.**

QUESTION: **How is a rabbit like a cornstalk?**
ANSWER: **They both have big ears.**

QUESTION: **When is an egg like a promise?**
ANSWER: **When it's broken.**

QUESTION: **Why is a baby like an old car?**
ANSWER: **Because they both have a rattle.**

QUESTION: **Why are pancakes like a baseball team?**
ANSWER: **Because they both need a good batter.**

Do you know any other simile jokes?

A good batter can make great pancakes or a great baseball team.

CHAPTER SEVEN

WHAT IS A METAPHOR?

DEFINITION

A **metaphor** compares two things by stating that one thing **is** the other thing.

Metaphors are very much like similes. They compare two different things that are alike in one important way. However, a metaphor doesn't use **like** or **as.** A metaphor says that one thing **is** something else! Here are some examples:

HOT TIP

Metaphor is pronounced "MET-uh-for."

EXAMPLE

Heather's **dress** was a **rainbow** of colors.
My **mind** is a **sponge** in science class.
Mr. Liu won't scold us. He's a real **cream puff.**

In each of these examples, a metaphor is used to compare the two green words. Those two things are alike in one important way:

SUBJECT	COMPARED TO	HOW THEY ARE ALIKE
dress	rainbow	Both are colorful.
mind	sponge	Both soak things up.
Mr. Liu	cream puff	Both are soft.

QUICK FACT
Metaphors

usually use a form of the verb to be. Those forms include am, is, are, was, and were.

TRY THESE!

Each sentence below contains a **metaphor.** Name the two things being compared. How are those two things alike?

1. Your computer is a doorway to the Internet.
2. Abbreviations for the states are an alphabet soup to me.
3. The recess bell was music to my ears.

See page 32 for the answers. Don't peek!

*This girl's **computer** is her **doorway** to the Internet. It is also her **window** to the world.*

CHAPTER EIGHT

CHICKENS, MONKEYS, AND HOGS

A nimals don't have good or bad attitudes in the same way that humans do. But people tend to see human qualities in animals. An animal's size or shape may suggest some quality, too. Some animal names have become common metaphors. Just look at these examples:

Are you silly? Do you make your friends laugh? If so, people might use a metaphor involving a monkey to describe you!

*Tipsy ate all the cat food. She is such a **hog**! She's really a kitten, but **hog** is used in a metaphor that describes eating too much.*

EXAMPLE

Are you afraid to dive off the high board?
You are a chicken!
Emily was a fish out of water at her
new school.
There's no cat food left because Tipsy is such
a hog.
The science fair was a whale of a good time.

Here are some animal names used in metaphors. Do you think

the quality given to each animal is fair or unfair?

ANIMAL	QUALITIES IN METAPHORS
bear	grouchy or heavily built
chameleon	changes ideas or personality often
chicken	fearful, cowardly
cold fish	unfriendly, not very nice
crab	grouchy
fish out of water	in an unfamiliar or uncomfortable situation
fox	clever, crafty
hog/pig	greedy, tends to take too much of something
monkey	fun, mischievous
porcupine	prickly, uncomfortable to be near
rat	unkind in a sneaky way
shark	takes advantage of others in a crafty way
snake	cannot be trusted, likely to betray others
weasel	sneaky, cannot be trusted
whale	big or impressive

CHAPTER NINE

LIFE IS JUST A
BOWL OF CHERRIES

Many songs and poems contain metaphors. Some of those metaphors have become common sayings. Some teach a lesson. Others show an unusual way of looking at things.

This girl is singing "You Are My Sunshine." It's a song based on a metaphor.

*Do you agree that **life** is just a **bowl of cherries**? If you do, you probably don't spend much time worrying about things!*

Here are a few examples:

EXAMPLE

METAPHOR: **No man is an island.**
MEANING: **All people are connected to one another.**

METAPHOR: **You are my sunshine.**
MEANING: **You are a bright spot in my life.**

METAPHOR: **All the world's a stage.**
MEANING: **We are all performing our parts in life.**

METAPHOR: **Life is just a bowl of cherries.**
MEANING: **You shouldn't take things too seriously.**

Do you agree with the messages in these metaphors? Why or why not?

CHAPTER TEN

THE WORLD IS YOUR OYSTER

Many other metaphors have become common sayings. Look on the next page for a few examples.

See the pearl inside this oyster? **The world is your oyster** *is a metaphor. It means you're free to explore the world and get things of value from it.*

METAPHOR: **Time is money.**

MEANING: **If you waste time, you are wasting money.**

METAPHOR: **The world is your oyster.**

MEANING: **You can use the world as you wish to get things of great value. Or, you can achieve anything.**

METAPHOR: **A man's home is his castle.**

MEANING: **People take pride in their homes and should be able to relax and enjoy themselves there.**

METAPHOR: **The eyes are the windows of the soul.**

MEANING: **People's eyes show their deepest thoughts and feelings.**

Do you agree with the messages in these metaphors? Why or why not?

*This woman looks quite happy eating ice cream and relaxing on her couch.
It's obvious that her **home** is her **castle**.*

How to Learn More

At the Library

Juster, Norton, and David Small (illustrator). *As: A Surfeit of Similes.* New York: Morrow Books, 1989.

Juster, Norton, and David Small (illustrator). *As Silly as Knees, as Busy as Bees.* New York: Beech Tree, 1998.

Tester, Sylvia R., and John Keely (illustrator). *You Dance like an Ostrich!: A Book of Similes.* Chicago: Children's Press, 1978.

On the Web

Visit our home page for lots of links about grammar:

http://www.childsworld.com/links

NOTE TO PARENTS, TEACHERS, AND LIBRARIANS: We routinely check our Web links to make sure they're safe, active sites—so encourage your readers to check them out!

Through the Mail or by Phone

To find the answer to a grammar question, contact:

THE GRAMMAR HOTLINE DIRECTORY
Tidewater Community College Writing Center, Building B205
1700 College Crescent
Virginia Beach, VA 23453
Telephone: (757) 822-7170

NATIONWIDE GRAMMAR HOTLINE
University of Arkansas at Little Rock, English Department
2801 South University Avenue
Little Rock, AR 72204-1099
Telephone: (501) 569-3161

Fun with Similes and Metaphors

Write a simile that compares each pair of words. Be sure to use **like** or **as.**

Example: mittens/kittens   My mittens are as furry as kittens.

1. dog/alarm clock

2. hair/bird's nest

3. feet/ice

4. cake/rock

Choose the meaning of each of these metaphors:

5. **Jonathan** was a **chicken** in the haunted house.

A. He was clucking. B. He was afraid. C. He had long legs.

6. **David** is a road **hog** when he rides his four-wheeler.

A. He is noisy. B. He grew up on a farm. C. He takes up too much road space.

7. **Tara** is an **ocean** of information.

A. She knows a lot. B. She is blue. C. She has some pet fish.

8. Our new **librarian** is a real **jewel.**

A. She shines in the sunlight. B. She is very valuable. C. She is expensive.

See page 32 for the answers. Don't peek!

Index

Answers

Answers to Text Exercises

page 7
1. (Lauren, mouse) Both are quiet.
2. (ocean, glass) Both are smooth.
3. (Ben, giraffe) Both have long, stretchy necks.

page 10
Answers will vary.

page 16
Answers will vary.

page 20
1. (computer, doorway) Both open up to something new.
2. (abbreviations, alphabet soup) Both contain lots of letters.
3. (recess bell, music) Both are welcome sounds.

Answers to Fun with Similes and Metaphors

1–4. Answers will vary.
5. B
6. C
7. A
8. B

About the Author

Ann Heinrichs was lucky. Every year from grade three through grade eight, she had a big, fat grammar textbook and a grammar workbook. She feels that this prepared her for life. She is now the author of more than 180 books for children and young adults. She has also enjoyed successful careers as a children's book editor and an advertising copywriter. Ann grew up in Fort Smith, Arkansas, and lives in Chicago, Illinois.